INTERNATIONAL LAW OF THE SEA – A PRIMER

[Every Student's Easy-to-Read Handbook of the Sea]

HENRIETTA NEWTON MARTIN

(B.com, LLB (Gold Medalist), LLM (Gold Medalist), MMS, etc)

This Book is dedicated to my God and Lord Yahweh, the Creator of Heaven and Earth, who alone is the source of all Wisdom;

& To my family of Newtons and Martins

Contents

Preface

Welcome to the International Law of The Sea- A Primer which is perspicuously crafted to the understanding of the students of law. International Law of the Sea is a part of Public International Law. The Law of the Sea regulates the relationship between states/countries in the matters pertaining to the sea and the waters by upholding three prominent principles, i.e. the principle of common heritage of mankind, principle of freedom and principle of sovereignty. The waters and seas are a free gift of nature and is expected to be legitimately used by the nations within the precincts of the law that governs and regulates the use and usage of the seas and international waters

This is the easy-to-read and easy-to-understand edition crafted to the level of understanding of students of international maritime law. It is endeavoured to keep the content as simple as possible; brevity in expression does not in any way mean a dearth of available material or that the allied topics are insignificant. The purpose of brevity is solely to encapsulate the principles adumbrated in this book in a perspicuous manner.

This easy-to-understand edition is a recommended must-have for every student of International Law and Maritime Law.

CHAPTER 1

The Law of the Sea-Introduction & Brief History

What Means the Law of the Sea?

As we all know the world depends on free trade, commerce, and effective communication. One of the modes of trade, transportation, and communication is by sea. In the 1400s big maritime powers were countries like Spain, Portugal, etc. Countries engaged in disputes over the international water zones claiming fishing zones etc. For instance, an additional 12 miles of the waters was claimed by Russia in the early 1900s as their fishing zone.

The principle here is the State that owns the surrounding land, desires to extend its right even to the adjacent and surrounding waters. So the Law of the Sea determines the extent of such dominance and parameters of sovereignty over the surrounding waters.

Early in the seventeenth century, Portugal claimed huge tracts of the high seas as part of their territorial domain. This claim was controverted and criticized by Dutch Statesman and scholar Hugo Grotius.

Thereby there was a need felt to address the squabbles, being snowballed into disputes, amidst other technological developments, exploitation of sea resources, need for prevention and conservation of marine resources, and thus the Law of the Sea developed over the years.

Hugo Grotius was considered the Father of International Law.

Mare Liberum (1609)

Hugo Grotius in his treatise Mare Liberum (1609) made mention of the need of regulating the seas by systemic law and opined that the "Law of the sea is a body of international law governing the rights and duties of states in maritime environments."

He expounded the doctrine of the open seas and opined that the oceans as 'res communis' and thus cannot be commonly appropriated and can be accessible to all nations. His work sparked criticism as well, nevertheless, it did result in the development of the law of the seas. He thereby propounded the concept of "free seas" and " freedom of navigation".

Law of the sea is that branch of the law that deals with the regulation of international waters, territorial waters, and maintaining public order; regulated by international covenants and treaties. It governs maritime commerce. It is a body of customs, treaties, international conventions, and agreements in matters pertaining to the sea with the purpose of maintaining peace and order among the nations.

It is a branch of codified international law, codifying the law regarding territorial waters, sea lanes, and resources.

Merriam Webster's Law Dictionary defines the law of the sea as "a body of international law promulgated by United Nations convention and covering a range of ocean matters including territorial zones, access to and transit on the sea, environmental preservation, and the resolution of international disputes."

The Law of the Sea Convention of 1958 served as a precursor to the development of codified law in this area.

The Law of the Sea Convention (LOSC) encompasses within its ambit three other conventions wiz:

1. Convention on the Territorial Sea and the Contiguous Zone;
2. Convention on the High Seas
   and
3. Convention on the Fishing and Conservation of Resources of the High Seas.

The United Nations Convention on the Law of the Sea was signed on December 10, 1982, and came into force in 1994 with the requisite number of 60 nations (117 for a start) acceding to the terms and ratifying the treaty. Later, more than 150 countries were made a party to the treaty upon ratification. It is worthwhile to note that the USA signed the agreement in 1994 but has not ratified it to date. However, it is a party to the 1956 convention, and follows other international customary provisions that may be reflective of the 1982 convention.' The UNCLOS operates as the 'Constitution' of the Law of the Sea.

It necessitates equitable and optimum-efficient utilization of the sea as a resource and the resources of the sea.

Before we delve into further, let us first understand what means territorial seas.

Territorial seas are distinct from High Seas.

The treaty UNCLOS defines territorial waters as "those extending 12 nautical mi (22 km) beyond a country's coast from the baseline (low water mark) and gives to each country exclusive fishing and mining rights in waters extending to 200 nautical miles (370 km) from its coast."

Territorial seas are thus waters that are immediately adjacent to the country's (State) territory/shores of the State and are subject to the authority and governance of that State. Trespassing over the waters is not permitted but the other State parties – its vessels may have the right of innocent passage, which means an authorized passage over the waters in compliance with international law and with all protocols followed.

What means contiguous zones?

Contiguous zones are where additional water stretches beyond the

limit/outer edge of the territorial sea, 24 nautical miles (44 km approx.) from the baseline within which the State exercises control and inflicts punishment for the infringement of its territorial limits, the relevant laws, and regulations. The State can exercise its power over these contiguous zones to prevent or punish trespass over its waters and infringement of relevant provisions of the law and regulations granting it right over the waters. Examples are Straits, canals, etc. Thereby in these zones, the special limited jurisdiction of the relevant State prevails.

What are Internal Waters?

The area within which the State exercises complete sovereignty over the water. Example – Rivers, Lakes, etc. The right of innocent passage is not granted to foreign vessels. However, if they must enter they are required to follow protocols and seek necessary permissions. In case of such inadvertent trespassing or negligence, foreign vessels are made subject to the domestic laws of the coastal state. The relevant port is granted the authority to incarcerate the foreign vessel for infringement of the law. In the case of disruption to peace and order as a consequence of such a foreign passage then criminal action may be initiated depending on the facts and circumstances of the case.

In Wildenhu's case 120 U.S. 1 (1887)

Wildenhus was a crewmember on board a Belgian ship, who was a Belgian national. The Belgian ship was docked at Jersey City in the United States. He killed a Belgian national, a fellow crewmember onboard the ship.

The US court used the principle prevalent under the then-relevant law that "when a matter is of such a nature as to disturb the peace and tranquillity of the local State, that State's authorities may exercise jurisdiction over the matter without interference from the home State", and thus adjudicated the matter. This case sought to approve concurrent jurisdiction in certain matters that may involve cases that affect the peace and order of a given state.

What are High Seas?

Waters beyond the territorial seas are international waters or the High sea over which every nation/State can freely use. However illegal activities and criminal activities are forbidden and would constitute an international offense. Examples: Piracy, Slave trade, etc. Every nation/State has got a right to sail its vessel flying its flag, over the high seas

High Sea is defined by Merriam-Webster's Dictionary as "the open ocean, especially that not within any country's jurisdiction". They are also classified as ABNJ i.e. Areas Beyond National Jurisdiction.

The Primary Dual Function of the LOS-Law of Sea

The primary function is the dissemination of authority over the waters/seas, i.e. internal waters/sea, territorial seas, contiguous zones, and high seas eliciting international cooperation between states.

Encourages international cooperation over matters pertaining to seas and the management of resources.

CHAPTER 2

Maritime Areas and Innocent Passage

Justice Oliver Wendell Holmes Jr. is said to have remarked once that, "the life of the law has not been logic: it has been experience.". International Law of the Sea seems to have been built around this premise and emerged as a law of consensus among nations. Law of the Sea binds the international community to a given maritime regime set forth under the international conventions primarily UNCLOS 1982.

The General Maritime Areas

1. **Internal Waters** is water over which the State exercises complete sovereignty, just as we discussed in the last chapter.
2. **The territorial sea** is that portion of the ocean where the State exercises sovereignty but there exists a right of innocent passage for foreign vessels without harming the rights of the State over the territorial sea. The territorial sea extends up to 12 nautical miles from the baseline (low water mark).
3. **Contiguous zones**, are zones that measure from the end of the 12 nautical miles of the territorial sea up to 24 nautical miles (44kms approx.), thus forming a contiguous zone. Example Canals, Straits

4. **International Straits:** The Commander's Handbook on the Law of Naval Operations (NWP 9) has defined a strait and conveyed that "straits are used for international navigation between one part of the high seas or an exclusive economic zone and another part of the high seas or an exclusive economic zone". The definition is derived from UNCLOS 1982, articles 37 and 38 of 1982. The Free Dictionary defines 'International Straits' as "an outlet from enclosed seas to the high seas that have a special legal status. The rules of navigation in such straits are regulated by special international agreements that in many cases contain restrictions on entry into enclosed seas by warships of countries without coastlines on those seas". Thereby the two factors about straits that come to the fore are 1. Their ability to connect water bodies and 2. The use of these straits for navigation. Thus, straits operate as international transit passages.
5. **EEZ** – Exclusive Economic Zone/Maritime Continental Margin- The UNCLOS 1982 defined the EEZ as "an area of the sea in which a sovereign state has special rights regarding the exploration and use of marine resources, including energy production from water and wind; and it stretches from the outer limit of the territorial sea (12 nautical miles from the baseline) out to 200 nautical miles (nmi) from the coast of the state in question". EEZ is an area adjacent to the territorial

sea, extending up to 200 nmi (370 km) out from its coastal baseline. Thereby the contiguous zones may come within the EEZ as well. It may even encompass artificial islands. The States have jurisdiction over the resources of the area under the EEZ. It is used for exploitation, extraction, conservation, and tapping of all living and non-living resources of the sea such as fishing, tapping sea minerals, Oil and Gas, allied resources, etc.

6. **Continental Shelf/Ocean Floor**- It is an area that lies towards the edge of a continent in the water where much of the exploring and exploitation of resources takes place. The continental margin comprises three components, i.e. continental rise, continental slope, and continental shelf. In this area called the continental shelf, most of the tapping/extraction of resources takes place. "It is a portion of a continent that is submerged under an area of relatively shallow water, known as a shelf sea".
7. **High Seas** – are classified as ABNJ i.e. Areas Beyond National Jurisdiction, which forms an extra-territorial space beyond the territorial seas and state jurisdiction.
8. Waters beyond the territorial seas are international waters or the High sea over which every nation/State can freely use, as Grotius advised that the sea is no man's property and can be freely used by anyone and everyone as a natural resource. However, UNCLOS 1982 tailored the right to the

effect to encourage the legitimate use of resources and the use of the sea for transit. In A. 87 (2) of the convention it generally restricts the freedom and states that it "must be exercised with appropriate respect for the interests of other Nations in their practice of high seas liberty." Illegal activities and criminal activities are forbidden and would constitute an international offense. Examples: Piracy, Slave trade, etc. Every nation/State has got a right to sail its vessel flying its flag, over the high seas. High Sea is defined by Merriam-Webster's Dictionary as "the open ocean, especially that not within any country's jurisdiction".

9. **Archipelagic waters**- An archipelago is a chain of islands spread across an area. Examples – Andaman and Nicobar Islands, Lakshadweep Island of India, the Hawaiian Islands, the Canary Islands, etc. The waters/the sea that surrounds the archipelagos are termed archipelagic waters. As per UNCLOS A.47, "An archipelagic State may draw straight archipelagic baselines joining the outermost points of the outermost islands and drying reefs of the archipelago provided that within such baselines are included the main islands and an area in which the ratio of the area of the water to the area of the land, including atolls, is between 1 to 1 and 9 to 1. The length of such baselines shall not exceed 100 nautical miles, except that up to 3 percent of the total number of baselines enclosing any archipelago

may exceed that length, up to a maximum length of 125 nautical miles". And further in A. 48 it states that – "The breadth of the territorial sea, the contiguous zone, the exclusive economic zone, and the continental shelf shall be measured from archipelagic baselines drawn, as stipulated in article 47".

Innocent Passage

The foundational principle upon which the doctrine of innocent passage is rooted is that the sea and its resource is a natural resource and is thereby to be made accessible to every human. It propagates freedom of navigation.

However, in modern and contemporary philosophy upon which the law of the sea has evolved; the sea is amenable to the sovereignty of the country around or in which it flows, and thereby the coastal country/state can impose legitimate restrictions on free use to the extent of avoiding illegal activities or activities that are detrimental to the peace and sovereignty of the coastal state and may require certain obligations and protocols to be met by the foreign ships/vessels before they enter the territorial waters.

The right of passage is a fundamental right that is granted under the international law of the sea, practiced under the sufferance of the coastal state through whose waters the foreign vessel sails. It can be considered as deemed sufferance by the coastal state for international passage subject to legitimate restrictions. Prior notifications may have to be provided depending upon the jurisdiction of the coastal state by the foreign ships before entering certain territorial waters, for example – UAE, Maldives, etc.

Some coastal ate require prior notification and authorization to be sought before entering their territorial waters example, Oman, Seychelles, etc. Some countries prohibit the use of their territorial seas for the transportation of mass destruction weapons. Example Lithuania and Romania. Some countries have prohibited the transportation of waste and refuse in their territorial waters with the apprehension of spills and consequent pollution. Example Haiti. In the case of foreign warships (naval ships, or vessels that may be engaged in war or carrying ammunitions of war), some countries require notification for the use of their territorial waters example India, Croatia, and Egypt. Some countries require notification and authorization/permission in case of warships passage – for example, UAE, Oman, etc

Thus, passage here is in terms of foreign vessels using the passage/a particular route via the territorial waters, or even the high seas subject to certain restrictions. Foreign submarines are required to navigate at the surface of the sea while passing through the territorial seas.

If the foreign vessel uses the passage for any criminal activity or in a way causes threat or there is a use of force or an act that disturbs the peace and tranquillity of a specific coastal state then such an act would be considered a violation of international law as stipulated in the UN Charter. Thereby passage will be considered as 'innocent' so far as nefarious or illegal activity is avoided. Thus, foreign ships are allowed peaceful entry and navigation into the territorial waters of another state except in circumstances that may be considered abusive of the rights of the coastal state and detrimental to its peace and security.

Article 17 of the UNCLOS III defines the right of innocent passage as "Subject to this Convention, ships of all States, whether coastal or land-locked, enjoy the right of innocent passage through the territorial sea"

The general definition that is attributed to the term 'Passage' by UNCLOS:

A. 18 of UNCLOS III defines passage as – "1. navigation through the territorial sea for the purpose of (a) traversing that sea without entering internal waters or calling at a roadstead or port facility outside internal waters; or

(b) proceeding to or from internal waters or a call at such roadstead or port facility.

2. Passage shall be continuous and expeditious. However, passage includes stopping and anchoring, but only in so far as the same are incidental to ordinary navigation or are rendered necessary by force majeure or distress or to assist persons, ships, or aircraft in danger or distress.

The Convention forbids any act or use of a weapon of any kind on board the vessel; any act that would be considered prejudicial to the defense or security of the coastal State, the landing, take off, or taking on board of any aircraft, any military device; the loading or unloading of any commodity/goods/currency in defiance with customs, fiscal, immigration or sanitary laws and regulations of the coastal State; any wilful act with the intention cause pollution; any specifically forbidden fishing activities; specifically forbidden research or survey activities; any act that interferes with communication systems or communication installations of the coastal State; or any other activity detrimental to the coastal state that is forbidden or would have an adverse impact on the coastal state.

A direct presumption is drawn that the navigation of the foreign vessel is peaceful and innocent unless proved contrary by the coastal state. The States can nevertheless limit the wide interpretation and usage of this law with their domestic laws under the rule of sovereignty as exercising jurisdiction over the territorial waters.

As per the Law of the Sea Convention of 1958, the coastal states can suspend innocent passage in certain designated areas in their control and at their legitimate discretion. Some countries do not permit innocent passage over territorial waters- For example Saudi Arabia.

Thereby it all depends upon each coastal state's promulgations over the use of their territorial waters in the exercise of their sovereignty over the territorial waters.

CHAPTER 3

Freedom of Navigation – FON

Freedom of navigation is an indispensable part of Law of the Sea.

It is the foundation stone of law of the sea. One of the purposes of law of the sea is to ensure peaceful navigation.

The Meriam Webster's Dictionary defines FON as "the right recognized in international law especially by treaties or agreements for vessels of one or all states to navigate streams passing through two or more states."

The 'Oscar Chinn Case'

[(Britain v. Belgium). [1934], P.C.I.J. (Ser. A/B) No. 63]

Permanent Court of International Justice (PCJ) December 12, 1934. |defined FON as "freedom of movement for vessels, freedom to enter ports and to make use of plant and docks, to load and unload goods and to transport goods and passengers."

Dupuy & Vignes in their 1991 treatise, at p. 836 opine that "Freedom of navigation (FON) is a principle of law of the sea that ships flying the flag of any sovereign state shall not suffer interference from other states, apart from the exceptions provided for in international law."

FON codified:

FON is a right that is codified under A.87 and A.90 of UNCLOS – United Nation Convention on Law of Seas.

A. 87 specifically states that under the clause - Freedom of the high seas; that -

1. The high seas are open to all States, whether coastal or land locked. Freedom of the high seas is exercised under the conditions laid down by this Convention and by other rules of international law.

It comprises, inter alia, both for coastal and land-locked States:

(a) freedom of navigation;

(b) freedom of overflight;

(c) freedom to lay submarine cables and pipelines, subject to Part VI; [VI of UNCLOS deals with continental shelf]

(d) freedom to construct artificial islands and other installations permitted under international law, subject to Part VI;

(e) freedom of fishing, subject to the conditions laid down in section 2;

(f) freedom of scientific research, subject to Parts VI (continental shelf) and XIII (Marine Scientific Research).

2. These freedoms shall be exercised by all States with due regard for the interests of other States in their exercise of the freedom of the high seas, and also with

due regard for the rights under this Convention with respect to activities in the Area.

Article 90 deals with the right of navigation

Every State, whether coastal or land-locked, has the right to sail ships flying its flag on the high seas.

International Law of the sea evolved over the years thereby concretizing the right of the freedom of navigation – FON; further the right evolved with its operational ramifications that led to the concept of Freedom of Navigation Operations (FONOPs); which operational freedom is based on sovereignty and interdependence of the state to enforce such a right.

CHAPTER 4

High Seas & UNCLOS

High Seas Definition

Merriam Dictionary defines High Sea as "the open part of a sea or ocean especially outside territorial waters."

The Fee Dictionary defines High Sea as, "The open waters of an ocean or a sea beyond the limits of the territorial jurisdiction of a country."

High Seas as defined in Britannica "high seas, in maritime law, is all parts of the mass of saltwater surrounding the globe that are not part of the territorial sea or internal waters of a state."

Thereby High seas are the portion of the open sea which are beyond the territorial waters or beyond jurisdiction of any state.

UNCLOS & High Seas

Chapter 7 of the United Nation Convention on the Law of the Sea deals with 'High Seas'. That apart Article 65 mentions about management and conservation of marine mammals in the high seas.

As per A.86 high seas encompass "all parts of the sea that are not included in the exclusive economic zone, in the territorial sea or in the internal waters of a State, or in the archipelagic waters of an archipelagic State."

A. 88 specifically entails peaceful use of the high seas, to the extent that it emphasizes the need for the high seas to be reserved for peaceful use or to be used for peaceful purposes.

A. 89 enumerates that no state/nation can claim sovereignty over the high seas.

Article 87 is a foundational article of chapter 7 of UNCLOS, which deals with the Freedom of the high seas.

It states that:

"1. The high seas are open to all States, whether coastal or land locked. Freedom of the high seas is exercised under the conditions laid down by this Convention and by other rules of international law. It comprises, inter alia, both for coastal and land-locked States:

(a) freedom of navigation;

(b) freedom of overflight;

(c) freedom to lay submarine cables and pipelines, subject to Part VI;

(d) freedom to construct artificial islands and other installations permitted under international law, subject to Part VI;

(e) freedom of fishing, subject to the conditions laid down in section 2;

(f) freedom of scientific research, subject to Parts VI and XIII.

2. These freedoms shall be exercised by all States with due regard for the interests of other States in their exercise of the freedom of the high seas, and also with due regard for the rights under this Convention with respect to activities in the Area."

Article 90 refers to Right of navigation

"Every State, whether coastal or land-locked, has the right to sail ships flying its flag on the high seas."

Article 91 deals with Nationality of ships

"1. Every State shall fix the conditions for the grant of its nationality to ships, for the registration of ships in its territory, and for the right to fly its flag. Ships have the nationality of the State whose flag they are entitled to fly. There must exist a genuine link between the State and the ship.

2. Every State shall issue to ships to which it has granted the right to fly its flag documents to that effect."

Article 92. Status of ships

"1. Ships shall sail under the flag of one State only and, save in exceptional cases expressly provided for in international treaties or in this Convention, shall be subject to its exclusive jurisdiction on the high seas. A ship may not change its flag during a voyage or while in a port of call, save in the case of a real transfer of ownership or change of registry.

2. A ship which sails under the flags of two or more States, using them according to convenience, may not claim any of the nationalities in question with respect to any other State, and may be assimilated to a ship without nationality."

Article 93. Refers to ships flying the flag of the UNO

Ships flying the flag of the United Nations, its specialized agencies and the International Atomic Energy Agency need to comply with the preceding provisions as well.

Article 94. Duties of the flag State

"1. Every State shall effectively exercise its jurisdiction and control in administrative, technical and social matters over ships flying its flag.

2. In particular every State shall:

(a) maintain a register of ships containing the names and particulars of ships flying its flag, except those which are excluded from generally accepted international regulations on account of their small size; and

(b) assume jurisdiction under its internal law over each ship flying its flag and its master, officers and crew in respect of administrative, technical and social matters concerning the ship."

3. 'Every State shall take such measures for ships flying its flag as are necessary to ensure safety at sea with regard, inter alia, to:

(a) the construction, equipment and seaworthiness of ships;

(b) the manning of ships, labour conditions and the training of crews, considering the applicable international instruments;

(c) the use of signals, the maintenance of communications and the prevention of collisions.

4. Such measures shall include those necessary to ensure:

(a) that each ship, before registration and thereafter at appropriate intervals, is surveyed by a qualified surveyor of ships, and has on board such charts, nautical publications and navigational equipment and instruments as are appropriate for the safe navigation of the ship

(b) that each ship is in the charge of a master and officers who possess appropriate qualifications, in particular in seamanship, navigation, communications and marine engineering, and that the crew is appropriate in qualification and numbers for the type, size, machinery and equipment of the ship;

"(c) that the master, officers and, to the extent appropriate, the crew are fully conversant with and required to observe the applicable international regulations concerning the safety of life at sea, the prevention of collisions, the prevention, reduction and control of marine pollution, and the maintenance of communications by radio.

5. In taking the measures called for in paragraphs 3 and 4 each State is required to conform to generally accepted international regulations, procedures and practices and to take any steps which may be necessary to secure their observance.

6. A State which has clear grounds to believe that proper jurisdiction and control with respect to a ship have not been exercised may report the facts to the flag State. Upon receiving such a report, the flag State shall investigate the matter and, if appropriate, take any action necessary to remedy the situation.

7. Each State shall cause an inquiry to be held by or before a suitably qualified person or persons into every marine casualty or incident of navigation on the high seas involving a ship flying its flag and causing loss of life or serious injury to nationals of another State or serious damage to ships or installations of another State or to the marine environment. The flag State and the other State shall co-operate in the conduct of any inquiry held by that other State into any such marine casualty or incident of navigation."

Article 95. Immunity of warships on the high seas are guaranteed, as against the jurisdiction of any other state other than the flag state.

Article 96. Immunity of ships used only on government noncommercial service

"Ships owned or operated by a State and used only on government non-commercial service shall, on the high seas, have complete immunity from the jurisdiction of any State other than the flag State."

Article 97. Penal jurisdiction in matters of collision or any other incident of navigation

"1. In the event of a collision or any other incident of navigation concerning a ship on the high seas, involving the penal or disciplinary responsibility of the master or of any other person in the service of the ship, no penal or disciplinary proceedings may be instituted against such person except before the judicial or administrative authorities either of the flag State or of the State of which such person is a national.

2. In disciplinary matters, the State which has issued a master's certificate or a certificate of competence or licence shall alone be competent after due legal process, to pronounce the withdrawal of such certificates, even if the holder is not a national of the State which issued them.

3. No arrest or detention of the ship, even as a measure of investigation, shall be ordered by any authorities other than those of the flag State."

Article 98. Duty to render assistance

"1. Every State shall require the master of a ship flying its flag, in so far as he can do so without serious danger to the ship, the crew or the passengers;

(a) to render assistance to any person found at sea in danger of being lost;

(b) to proceed with all possible speed to the rescue of persons in distress, if informed of their need of assistance, in so far as such action may reasonably be expected of him;

(c) after a collision, to render assistance to the other ship, its crew and its passengers and, where possible, to inform the other ship of the name of his own ship, its port of registry and the nearest port at which it will call.

2. Every coastal State shall promote the establishment, operation and maintenance of an adequate and effective search and rescue service regarding safety on and over the sea and, where circumstances so require, by way of mutual regional arrangements co-operate with neighbouring States for this purpose."

Article 99. Prohibition of the transport of slaves

"Every State shall take effective measures to prevent and punish the transport of slaves in ships authorized to fly its flag and to prevent the unlawful use of its flag for that purpose. Any slave taking refuge on board any ship, whatever its flag, shall ipso facto be free."

Article 109. Unauthorized broadcasting from the high seas

"1. All States shall co-operate in the suppression of unauthorized broadcasting from the high seas.

2. For the purposes of this Convention, 'unauthorized broadcasting' means the transmission of sound radio or

television broadcasts from a ship or installation on the high seas intended-for reception by the general public contrary to international regulations, but excluding the transmission of distress calls.

3. Any person engaged in unauthorized broadcasting may be prosecuted before the court of:

(a) the flag State of the ship;

(b) the State of registry of the installation;

(c) the State of which the person is a national;

(d) any State where the transmissions can be received; or

(e) any State where authorized radio communication is suffering interference.

4. On the high seas, a State having jurisdiction in accordance with clause 3 may, in conformity with article 110, arrest any person or ship engaged in unauthorized broadcasting and seize the broadcasting apparatus."

Article 110. Right of visit

"1. Except where acts of interference derive from powers conferred by treaty, a warship which encounters on the high seas a foreign ship, other than a ship entitled to complete immunity in accordance with articles 95 and 96, is not justified in boarding it unless there is reasonable ground for suspecting that:

(a) the ship is engaged in piracy;

(b) the ship is engaged in the slave trade;

(c) the ship is engaged in unauthorized broadcasting and the flag

State of the warship has jurisdiction under article 109;

(d) the ship is without nationality; or

(e) though flying a foreign flag or refusing to show its flag, the ship is, in reality, of the same nationality as the warship."

"2. In the cases provided for in paragraph 1, the warship may proceed to verify the ship's right to fly its flag. To this end, it may send a boat under the command of an officer to the suspected ship. If suspicion remains after the documents have been checked, it may proceed to a further examination on board the ship, which must be carried out with all possible consideration.

3. If the suspicions prove to be unfounded, and provided that the ship boarded has not committed any act justifying them, it shall be compensated for any loss or damage that may have been sustained.

4. These provisions apply mutatis mutandis (as per changing circumstances) to military aircraft.

5. These provisions also apply to any other duly authorized ships or aircraft clearly marked and identifiable as being on government service."

Article 111. Right of hot pursuit

“1. The hot pursuit of a foreign ship may be undertaken when the competent authorities of the coastal State have good reason to believe that the ship has violated the laws and regulations of that State. Such pursuit must be commenced when the foreign ship or one of its boats is within the internal waters, the archipelagic waters, the territorial sea or the contiguous zone of the pursuing State, and may only be continued outside the territorial sea or the contiguous zone if the pursuit has not been interrupted. It is not necessary that, at the time when the foreign ship within the territorial sea or the contiguous zone receives the order to stop, the ship giving the order should likewise be within the territorial sea or the contiguous zone. If the foreign ship is within a contiguous zone, as defined in article 33, the pursuit may only be undertaken if there has been a violation of the rights for the protection of which the zone was established. 2. The right of hot pursuit shall apply mutatis mutandis” (adapt to changes, make changes as per the change) “to violations in the exclusive economic zone or on the continental shelf, including safety zones around continental shelf installations, of the laws and regulations of the coastal State applicable per this Convention to the exclusive economic zone or the continental shelf, including such safety zones.

3. The right of hot pursuit ceases as soon as the ship pursued enters the territorial sea of its own State or of a third State.

4. Hot pursuit is not deemed to have begun unless the pursuing ship has satisfied itself by such practicable means as may be available that the ship pursued or one of its boats or other craft working as a team and using the ship pursued as a mother ship is within the limits of the territorial sea, or, as the case may be, within the contiguous zone or the exclusive economic zone or above the continental shelf. The pursuit may only be commenced after a visual or auditory signal to stop has been given at a distance which enables it to be seen or heard by the foreign ship.

5. The right of hot pursuit may be exercised only by warships or military aircraft, or other ships or aircraft clearly marked and identifiable as being on government service and authorized to that effect."

6. Where hot pursuit is affected by an aircraft:

(a) the provisions of paragraphs 1 to 4 shall apply mutatis mutandis (make amends as per changing circumstances);

(b) the aircraft giving the order to stop must actively pursue the ship until a ship or another aircraft of the coastal State, summoned by the aircraft, arrives to take over the pursuit unless the aircraft is itself able to arrest the ship. It does not suffice to justify an arrest outside the territorial sea that the ship was merely sighted by the aircraft as an offender or suspected offender if it was not both ordered to stop and pursued by the aircraft itself or other aircraft or ships that continue the pursuit without interruption."

7. The release of a ship arrested within the jurisdiction of a State and escorted to a port of that State for an inquiry before the competent authorities may not be claimed solely on the ground that the ship, in the course of its voyage, was escorted across a portion of the exclusive economic zone or the high seas, if the circumstances rendered this necessary.

8. Where a ship has been stopped or arrested outside the territorial sea in circumstances which do not justify the exercise of the right of hot pursuit, it shall be compensated for any loss or damage that may have been thereby sustained."

Article 112. Right to lay submarine cables and pipelines

"1. All States are entitled to lay submarine cables and pipelines on the bed of the high seas beyond the continental shelf.

2. Article 79, paragraph 5, applies to such cables and pipelines.

[Article 79 (2) stipulates that: "Subject to its right to take reasonable measures for the exploration of the continental shelf, the exploitation of its natural resources and the prevention, reduction and control of pollution from pipelines, the coastal State may not impede the laying or maintenance of such cables or pipelines"

Cross reference to A. 4 of Law of Sea Convention where this principle was originally crafted and incorporated in the draft."

Article 113. Breaking or injury of a submarine cable or pipeline

“Every State shall adopt the laws and regulations necessary to provide that the breaking or injury by a ship flying its flag or by a person subject to its jurisdiction of a submarine cable beneath the high seas done willfully or through culpable negligence, in such a manner as to be liable to interrupt or obstruct telegraphic or telephonic communications, and similarly the breaking or in jury of a submarine pipeline or high-voltage power cable, shall be a punishable offence. This provision shall apply also to conduct calculated or likely to result in such breaking or injury. However, it shall not apply to any break or injury caused by persons who acted merely with the legitimate object of saving their lives or their ships, after having taken all necessary precautions to avoid such break or in jury.”

Article 114. Breaking or injury by owners of a submarine cable or pipeline of another submarine cable or pipeline

“Every State shall adopt the laws and regulations necessary to provide that, if persons subject to its jurisdiction who are owners of a submarine cable or pipeline beneath the high seas, in laying or repairing that cable or pipeline, cause a break m or injury to another cable or pipeline, they shall bear the cost of the repairs.”

Article 115. Indemnity for loss incurred in avoiding injury to a submarine cable or pipeline

"Every State shall adopt the laws and regulations necessary to ensure that the owners of ships who can prove that they have sacrificed an anchor, a net or any other fishing gear, in order to avoid injuring a submarine cable or pipeline, shall be indemnified by the owner of the cable or pipeline, provided that the owner of the ship has taken all reasonable precautionary measures beforehand."

Section 2 f Part 7 of UNCLOS deals with conservation of living resources in the high seas.

Article 116. Right to fish on the high seas

"All States have the right for their nationals to engage in fishing on the high seas subject to:

(a) their treaty obligations;

(b) the rights and duties as well as the interests of coastal States provided for, inter alia, in article 63, paragraph 2, and articles 64 to 67; and

(c) the provisions of this section."

Article 117. Duty of States to adopt national measures for the conservation of the living resources of the high seas

"All States have the duty to take, or to co-operate with other States in taking, such measures for their respective nationals as may be necessary for the conservation of the living resources of the high seas."

Article 118. Co-operation of States in the conservation and management of living resources

"States shall co-operate with each other in the conservation and management of living resources in the areas of the high seas. States whose nationals exploit identical living resources, or different living resources m the same area, shall enter into negotiations with a view to taking the measures necessary for the conservation of the living resources concerned. They shall, as appropriate, co-operate to establish sub regional or regional fisheries organizations to this end."

Article 119. Conservation of the living resources of the high seas

"1. In determining the allowable catch and establishing other conservation measures for the living resources in the high seas, States shall:

(a) take measures which are designed, on the best scientific evidence available to the States concerned, to maintain or restore populations of harvested species at levels which can produce the maximum sustainable yield, as qualified by relevant environmental and economic factors, including the special requirements of developing States, and taking into account fishing patterns, the interdependence of stocks and any generally recommended international minimum standards, whether sub-regional, regional or global;

(b) take into consideration the effects on species associated with or dependent upon harvested species with a view to maintaining or restoring populations of such associated or dependent species above levels at which their reproduction may become seriously threatened."

2. Available scientific information, catch and fishing effort statistics, and other data relevant to the conservation of fish stocks shall be contributed and exchanged on a regular basis through competent international organizations, whether sub regional, regional or global, where appropriate and with participation by all States concerned.

3. States concerned shall ensure that conservation measures and their implementation do not discriminate in form or in fact against the fishermen of any State. "

Article 120 deals with the protection of Marine mammals, and A.65 deals with the conservation and management of marine mammals in the high seas.

And lastly A. 100 to A. 108, 110 deals with piracy which will be discussed in the next chapter.

BBNJ Treaty 2023 complements the UNCLOS

On 20 September 2023, the United Nations High Seas Treaty, also known as the Biodiversity Beyond National Jurisdiction Treaty was signed in New York in the margins of the United Nations High-Level Week, also called as the BBNJ treaty. The BBNJ treaty is a promising move in the conservation and regulation of the High Seas. This is a legally binding instrument for the conservation and sustainable use of marine biological diversity in areas beyond national jurisdiction. 84 countries are signatories to this treaty.

CHAPTER 5

Piracy – An International Crime

Piracy - Meaning and UNCLOS

Piracy is a maritime crime that endangers maritime security and the welfare of the vessels sailing on the high seas.

Piracy simply means robbery on the high seas. In legal parlance, piracy can include activities such as robbery, kidnapping, and criminal intimidation on board with a robbery at gunpoint, etc.

The area beyond the territorial seas of 12 nm is considered the high seas. When the robbery is committed within the territorial waters it would be adjudicated as per the domestic laws of the coastal state.

Thereby piracy is a crime committed on the high seas and comes within the ambit of international law. A pirate may be prosecuted under international laws or as per laws of the nation to which the pirate belongs or is a national.

Part VII of the United Nations Convention on the Law of the Sea -1982 deals with the offense of piracy under Articles 100 to 108 and 110.

Article 101. defines piracy as consisting of the following acts:

"(a) any illegal acts of violence or detention, or any act of depredation, committed for private ends by the crew or the passengers of a private ship or a private aircraft and directed:

(i) on the high seas, against another ship or aircraft, or against persons or property on board such ship or aircraft;

(ii) against a ship, aircraft, persons, or property in a place outside the jurisdiction of any State;

(b) any act of voluntary participation in the operation of a ship or of an aircraft with knowledge of facts making it a pirate ship or aircraft;

(c) any act of inciting or intentionally facilitating an act described in subparagraphs (a) or (b)

Article 100 deals with the duty to cooperate in the repression of piracy

It states – "All States shall cooperate to the fullest possible extent in the repression of piracy on the high seas or in any other place outside the jurisdiction of any State."

Article 102 refers to piracy by a warship, government ship, or government aircraft whose crew has mutinied

It specifically states that –" the acts of piracy, as defined in article 101, committed by a warship, government ship or government aircraft whose crew has mutinied and taken control of the ship or aircraft are assimilated to acts committed by a private ship or aircraft."

Article 103. Defines a pirate ship or aircraft

A ship or aircraft is considered a pirate ship or aircraft if it is intended by the persons in dominant control to be used for the purpose of committing one of the acts referred to in article 101. The same applies if the ship or aircraft has been used to commit any such act, so long as it remains under the control of the persons guilty of that act.

Article 104 specifies that retention or loss of the nationality of a pirate ship or aircraft is to be determined by Law.

Generally, a ship or aircraft may retain its nationality even if it is a pirate ship or aircraft. A.104 clearly states that – "... The retention or loss of nationality is determined by the law of the State from which such nationality was derived."

Article 105 deals with the seizure of a pirate ship or aircraft

It states " On the high seas, or in any other place outside the jurisdiction of any State, every State may seize a pirate ship or aircraft, or a ship or aircraft taken by piracy and under the control of pirates, and arrest the persons and seize the property on board. The courts of the State which carried out the seizure may decide upon the penalties to be imposed, and may also determine the action to be taken with regard to the ships, aircraft or property, subject to the rights of third parties acting in good faith."

Article 106 refers to the liability for seizure without adequate grounds

It states – "Where the seizure of a ship or aircraft on suspicion of piracy has been effected without adequate grounds, the State making the seizure shall be liable to the State the nationality of which is possessed by the ship or aircraft for any loss or damage caused by the seizure."

Article 107 deals with ships and aircraft which are entitled to seize on account of piracy

"A seizure on account of piracy may be carried out only by warships or military aircraft, or other ships or aircraft clearly marked and identifiable as being on government service and authorized to that effect."

Article 108 stipulates the cooperation of states in the case of Illicit traffic of narcotic drugs or psychotropic substances

1. All States shall cooperate in the suppression of illicit traffic in narcotic drugs and psychotropic substances engaged in by ships on the high seas contrary to international conventions.

2. Any State which has reasonable grounds for believing that a ship flying its flag is engaged in illicit traffic of

narcotic drugs or psychotropic substances may request the cooperation of other States to suppress such traffic.

Under **A.110 right of a visit is not permitted in case of ships engaged in piracy**.

CHAPTER 6

EEZ – Exclusive Economic Zones and UNCLOS-1982

An "Exclusive Economic Zone," or "EEZ" is an area of the ocean beyond 12 nautical miles of a nation's territorial sea baseline, extending up to 200 nautical miles. The coastal nation has jurisdiction over both living and nonliving resources of the EEZ. Article 57 of UNCLOS specifies the breadth of the exclusive economic zone, where it states that "the exclusive economic zone shall not extend beyond 200 nautical miles from the baselines from which the breadth of the territorial sea is measured."

Part V of the UNCLOS 1982, Articles 55 to 75, deals with the provisions pertinent to the Exclusive Economic Zone.

Article 55 provides for a specific legal regime for the exclusive economic zones.

It states – "The exclusive economic zone is an area beyond and adjacent to the territorial sea, subject to the specific legal regime established in this Part, under which the rights and jurisdiction of the coastal State and the rights and freedoms of other States are governed by the relevant provisions of this Convention."

Article 56. enumerates the rights, jurisdiction, and duties of the coastal State in the exclusive economic zone

It states that "1. In the exclusive economic zone, the coastal State has:

(a) sovereign rights for the purpose of exploring and exploiting, conserving and managing the natural resources, whether living or non-living, of the waters superjacent to the sea-bed and of the sea-bed and its subsoil, and with regard to other activities for the economic exploitation and exploration of the zone, such as the production of energy from the water, currents and winds;

(b) jurisdiction as provided for in the relevant provisions of this Convention with regard to:

(i) the establishment and use of artificial islands, installations and structures;

(ii) marine scientific research;

(iii) the protection and preservation of the marine environment;

(c) other rights and duties provided for in this Convention.

2. In exercising its rights and performing its duties under this Convention in the exclusive economic zone, the coastal State shall have due regard to the rights and duties of other States and shall act in a manner compatible with the provisions of this Convention.

3. The rights set out in this article with respect to the sea bed and subsoil shall be exercised in accordance with Part VI." Part VI deals with provisions relating to the continental shelf. "

Article 57 specifies the breadth of the exclusive economic zone

"The exclusive economic zone shall not extend beyond 200 nautical miles from the baselines from which the breadth of the territorial sea is measured."

Article 58 enumerates the rights and duties of other States in the exclusive economic zone

"1. In the exclusive economic zone, all States, whether coastal or land-locked, enjoy, subject to the relevant provisions of this Convention, the freedoms referred to in article 87 of navigation and overflight and of the laying of submarine cables and pipelines, and other internationally lawful uses of the sea related to these freedoms, such as those associated with the operation of ships, aircraft and submarine cables and pipelines, and compatible with the other provisions of this Convention."

2. Articles 88 to 115 (generally dealing with High Seas) and other pertinent rules of "international law apply to the exclusive economic zone in so far as they are not incompatible with this Part."

3. In exercising their rights and performing their duties under this Convention in the exclusive economic zone, States shall have due regard to the rights and duties of

the coastal State and shall comply with the laws and regulations adopted by the coastal State in accordance with the provisions of this Convention and other rules of international law in so far as they are not incompatible with this Part."

Article 59 deals with the basis for the resolution of conflicts regarding the attribution of rights and jurisdiction in the exclusive economic zone

It states "In cases where this Convention does not attribute rights or jurisdiction to the coastal State or to other States within the exclusive economic zone, and a conflict arises between the interests of the coastal State and any other State or States, the conflict should be resolved on the basis of equity and in the light of all the relevant circumstances, taking into account the respective importance of the interests involved to the parties as well as to the international community as a whole."

Article 60 provides for provisions governing artificial islands, installations, and structures in the exclusive economic zone

It reads – "1. In the exclusive economic zone, the coastal State shall have the exclusive right to construct and to authorize, and regulate the construction, operation and use of:

(a) artificial islands;

(b) installations and structures for the purposes provided for in article 56 and other economic purposes;

© installations and structures which may interfere with the exercise of the rights of the coastal State in the zone.

2. The coastal State shall have exclusive jurisdiction over such artificial islands, installations and structures, including jurisdiction with regard to customs, fiscal, health, safety, and immigration laws and regulations.

3. Due notice must be given of the construction of such artificial islands, installations or structures, and permanent means for giving warning of their presence must be maintained. Any installations or structures which are abandoned or disused shall be removed to ensure safety of navigation, taking into account any generally accepted international standards established in this regard by the competent international organization. Such removal shall also have due regard to fishing, the protection of the marine environment, and the rights and duties of other States. Appropriate publicity shall be given to the depth, position, and dimensions of any installations or structures not entirely removed.

4. The coastal State may, where necessary, establish reasonable safety zones around such artificial islands, installations, and structures in which it may take appropriate measures to ensure the safety both of navigation and of the artificial islands, installations, and, structures.

5. The breadth of the safety zones shall be determined by the coastal State, considering applicable international

standards. Such zones shall be designed to ensure that they are reasonably related to the nature and function of the artificial islands, installations, or structures, and shall not exceed a distance of 500 meters around, them, measured from each point of their outer edge, except an authorized by generally accepted international standards or a recommended by the competent international organization. Due notice shall be given of the extent of safety zones.

6. All ships must respect these safety zones and shall comply with generally accepted international standards regarding navigation in the vicinity of artificial islands, installations, structures, and safety zones.

7. Artificial islands, installations, and structures and the safety zone around them may not be established where interference may be caused to the use of recognized sea lanes essential to international navigation.

8. Artificial islands, installations, and structures do not possess the status of islands. They have no territorial sea of their own, and their presence does not affect the delimitation of the territorial sea, the exclusive economic zone or the continental shelf."

Article 61 deals with the conservation of the living resources in the EEZ

It states that – "1. The coastal State shall determine the allowable catch of the living resources in its exclusive economic zone.

2. The coastal State, taking into account the best scientific evidence available to it, shall ensure through proper conservation and management measures that the maintenance of the living resources in the exclusive economic zone is not endangered by over-exploitation. As appropriate, the coastal State and competent international organizations, whether sub-regional, regional, or global, shall cooperate to this end.

3. Such measures shall also be designed to maintain or restore populations of harvested species at a level that can produce the maximum sustainable yield, as qualified by relevant environmental and economic factors, including the economic needs of coastal fishing communities and the special requirements of developing States, and taking into account fishing patterns, the interdependence of stocks and any generally recommended international minimum standards, whether sub-regional, regional or global."

4. In taking such measures the coastal State shall take into consideration the effects on species associated with or dependent upon harvested species with a view to maintaining or restoring populations of such associated or dependent species above levels at which their reproduction may become seriously threatened.

5. Available scientific information, catch and fishing effort statistics, and other data relevant to the conservation of fish stocks shall be contributed and exchanged on a regular basis through competent international organizations, whether sub-regional, regional, or global,

where appropriate and with participation by all States concerned, including States whose nationals are allowed to fish in the exclusive economic zone."

Article 62 stipulates provisions relating to utilization of the living resources

"1. The coastal State shall promote the objective of optimum utilization of the living resources in the exclusive economic zone without prejudice to article 61.

2. The coastal State shall determine its capacity to harvest the living resources of the exclusive economic zone. Where the coastal State does not have the capacity to harvest the entire allowable catch, it shall, through agreements or other arrangements and pursuant to the terms, conditions, laws, and regulations referred to in paragraph 4, give other States access to the surplus of the allowable catch, having particular regard to the provisions of articles 69 and 70, especially in relation to the developing States mentioned therein."

3. In giving access to other States to its exclusive economic zone under this article, the coastal State shall take into account all relevant factors, including, inter alia, the significance of the living resources of the area to the economy of the coastal State concerned and its other national interests, the provisions of articles 69 and 70, the requirements of developing States in the subregion or region in harvesting part of the surplus and the need to minimize economic dislocation in States whose nationals have habitually fished in the zone or which have made

substantial efforts in research and identification of stocks."

4. Nationals of other States fishing in the exclusive economic zone shall comply with the conservation measures and with the other terms and conditions established in the laws and regulations of the coastal State. These laws and regulations shall be consistent with this Convention and may relate, inter alia, to the following:

(a) licensing of fishermen, fishing vessels and equipment, including payment of fees and other forms of remuneration, which, in the case of developing coastal States, may consist of adequate compensation in the field of financing, equipment and technology relating to the fishing industry;

(b) determining the species which may be caught, and fixing quotas of catch, whether in relation to particular stocks or groups of stocks or catch per vessel over a period of time or to the catch by nationals of any State during a specified period;

(c) regulating seasons and areas of fishing, the types, sizes and amount of gear, and the types, sizes and number of fishing vessels that may be used;

(d) fixing the age and size of fish and other species that may be caught;

(e) specifying information required of fishing vessels, including catch and effort statistics and vessel position reports;

(f) requiring, under the authorization and control of the coastal State, the conduct of specified fisheries research programmes and regulating the conduct of such research, including the sampling of catches, disposition of samples and reporting of associated scientific data;

(g) the placing of observers or trainees on board such vessels by the coastal State;

(h) the landing of all or any part of the catch by such vessels in the ports of the coastal State;

(i) terms and conditions relating to joint ventures or other cooperative arrangements;

(j) requirements for the training of personnel and the transfer of fisheries technology, including enhancement of the coastal State's capability of undertaking fisheries research;

(k) enforcement procedures.

5. Coastal States shall give due notice of conservation and management, laws, and regulations. "

Article 63. deals with the conservation of Stocks occurring within the exclusive economic zones of two or more coastal States or both within the exclusive economic zone and in an area beyond and adjacent to it.

Article 64 deals with the conservation of highly migratory species.

Article 65 deals with conservation and limiting the abuse and exploitation of Marine mammals towards which end the States shall cooperate along with international as well as inter-governmental organizations.

A. 66 deals with the conservation of anadromous stocks (for example Salmon fish) and its fishing in the EEZ. Anadromous stocks are those which migrate from the sea to the rivers to breed or spawn in fresh waters.

Article 67. deals with Catadromous species whose fishing is permitted only in inland waters. Catadromous species are those that spend their life cycle in rivers and fresh waters but breed/spawn in the sea. For example eel.

Article 69 specifies the right of land-locked States

It states that "1. Land-locked States shall have the right to participate, on an equitable basis, in the exploitation of an appropriate part of the surplus of the living resources of the exclusive economic zones of coastal States of the same subregion or region, taking into account the relevant economic and geographical circumstances of all the States concerned and in conformity with the provisions of this article and of articles 61 and 62...."

Article 70. Right of geographically disadvantaged States

"1. Geographically disadvantaged States shall have the right to participate, on an equitable basis, in the exploitation of an appropriate part of the surplus of the living resources of the exclusive economic zones of coastal States of the same subregion or region, taking into account the relevant economic and geographical circumstances of all the States concerned and in conformity with the provisions of this article and of articles 61 and 62.

2. For the purposes of this Part, 'geographically disadvantaged States' means coastal States, including States bordering enclosed or semi-enclosed seas, whose geographical situation makes them dependent upon the exploitation of the living resources of the exclusive economic zones of other States in the subregion or region for adequate supplies of fish for the nutritional purposes of their populations or parts thereof, and coastal States which can claim no exclusive economic zones of their own....."

Article 71 specifies about the Non-applicability of articles 69 and 70 in the " case of a coastal State whose economy is overwhelmingly dependent on the exploitation of the living resources of its exclusive economic zone."

Article 72. lays down the restrictions on transfer of rights

"1. Rights provided under articles 69 and 70 to exploit living resources shall not be directly or indirectly transferred to third States or their nationals by lease or licence, by establishing joint ventures or in any other manner which has the effect of such transfer unless otherwise agreed by the States concerned.

2. The foregoing provision does not preclude the States concerned from obtaining technical or financial assistance from third States or international organizations in order to facilitate the exercise of the rights pursuant

to articles 69 and 70, provided that it does not have the effect referred to in paragraph 1."

Article 71 specifies about the Non-applicability of articles 69 and 70 in the " case of a coastal State whose economy is overwhelmingly dependent on the exploitation of the living resources of its exclusive economic zone."

Article 72. lays down the restrictions on the transfer of rights

"1. Rights provided under articles 69 and 70 to exploit living resources shall not be directly or indirectly transferred to third States or their nationals by lease or license by establishing joint ventures or in any other manner which has the effect of such transfer unless otherwise agreed by the States concerned.

2. The foregoing provision does not preclude the States concerned from obtaining technical or financial assistance from third States or international organizations in order to facilitate the exercise of the rights pursuant to articles 69 and 70, provided that it does not have the effect referred to in paragraph 1."

Article 73. Enforcement of laws and regulations of the coastal State

1. The coastal State may, in the exercise of its sovereign rights to explore, exploit, conserve and manage the living resources in the exclusive economic zone, take such measures, including boarding, inspection, arrest and judicial proceedings, as may be necessary to ensure

compliance with the laws and regulations adopted by it in conformity with this Convention.

2. Arrested vessels and their crews shall be promptly released upon the posting of reasonable bond or other security.

3. Coastal State penalties for violations of fisheries laws and regulations in the exclusive economic zone may not include imprisonment, in the absence of agreements to the contrary by the States concerned, or any other form of corporal punishment.

4. In cases of arrest or detention of foreign vessels the coastal State shall promptly notify the flag State, through appropriate channels, of the action taken and of any penalties subsequently imposed.

Article 74. Delimitation of the exclusive economic zone between States with opposite or adjacent coasts

1. The delimitation of the exclusive economic zone between States with opposite or adjacent coasts shall be effected by agreement on the basis of international law as referred to in Article 38 of the Statute of the International Court of Justice, in order to achieve an equitable solution.

2. If no agreement can be reached within a reasonable period of time, the States concerned shall resort to the procedures provided for in Part XV.

3. Pending agreement as provided for in paragraph 1, the States concerned, in a spirit of understanding

and co-operation, shall make every effort to enter into provisional arrangements of a practical nature and, during this transitional period, not to jeopardize or hamper the reaching of the final agreement. Such arrangements shall be without prejudice to the final delimitation.

4. Where there is an agreement in force between the States concerned, questions relating to the delimitation of the exclusive economic zone shall be determined in accordance with the provisions of that agreement.

Article 75. Charts and lists of geographical co-ordinates

1. Subject to this Part, the outer limit lines of the exclusive economic zone and the lines of delimitation drawn in accordance with article 74 shall be shown on charts of a scale or scales adequate for ascertaining their position. Where appropriate, lists of geographical coordinates of points, specifying the geodetic datum, may be substituted for such outer limit lines or lines of delimitation.

2. The coastal State shall give due publicity to such charts or lists of geographical coordinates and shall deposit a copy of each such chart or list with the Secretary-General of the United Nations.

CHAPTER 7

Allied Conventions

The Convention on the High Seas 1958, effective 1962- 37 Articles in all.

This convention was part of the four treaties signed at the time of the United Nation Convention on the Law of the Sea- UNCLOS-I/LOS

Some of the important provisions of the treaty are as follows:

Article 1 defines the High Seas as meaning "all parts of the sea that are not included in the territorial sea or in the internal waters of a State."

Article 2 states that

"The high seas being open to all nations, no State may validly purport to subject any part of them to its sovereignty. Freedom of the high seas is exercised under the conditions laid down by these articles and by the other rules of international law. It comprises, inter alia, both for coastal and non-coastal States:

1. Freedom of navigation;
2. Freedom of fishing;

3. Freedom to lay submarine cables and pipelines;
4. Freedom to fly over the high seas.

These freedoms, and others which are recognized by the general principles of international law shall be exercised by all States with reasonable regard to the interests of other States in their exercise of the freedom of the high seas.

Article 4 specifies that "Every State, whether coastal or not, has the right to sail ships under its flag on the high seas."

Article 5 enumerates that every state shall fix conditions for granting nationality to the vessel/ships and registering ships within its territory. And thus every state shall effectively exercise jurisdiction and control over ships flying its flag, whether administrative, technical, or social.

Article 6 states, Ships shall sail under the flag of one State only and, save in exceptional

cases expressly provided for in international treaties. Further, a ship may not change its flag during a voyage or while in a port of call, except in the case of a real transfer of ownership or change of registry.

Articles 8 and 9

A. 8 states that "warships on the high seas have complete immunity from the jurisdiction of any State other than the flag State. " and A. 9 states that non –commercial ships have complete immunity as well from the jurisdiction of other states, except the flag state.

For the purposes of article 8, the term "warship" means "a ship belonging to the naval forces of a State and bearing the external marks distinguishing warships of its nationality, under the command of an officer duly commissioned by the government and whose name appears in the Navy List, and manned by a crew who are under regular naval discipline."

Transportation of slaves and other unlawful activity is forbidden under A.12.

A. 14 to 22 deals with piracy and forbids it.

The convention on the High Seas was superseded by the 1982 United Nation Convention on the Law of the Sea-UNCLOS III.

Conclusion:

Thereby there has been UNCLOS I (1958)/Law of the Sea Convention – LOSC 1958; under which four treaties were signed that is:

1. Convention on the High Seas
2. The Convention on the Territorial Sea and Contiguous Zone;
3. The Convention on Fishing and Conservation of the Living Resources of the High Seas; and
4. The Convention on the Continental Shelf.

There has been UNCLOS II in 1960 which did not succeed and failed to achieve international concurrence and treaties.

And the prominent one in force today is UNCLOS III – The 1982 Convention on the Law of the Sea.

CHAPTER 8

Dispute Resolution – LOS

Introduction

Conflicts and disputes under the law of the sea may be primarily addressed by way of settlement in a peaceful manner in compliance with the UN Charter, A.3.

However, if the matter remains unsettled, not capable of being negotiated and the matter did not culminate in the drawing of a settlement agreement then the dispute may be referred to the appropriate adjudicatory body established under the relevant law. Before seeking adjudication under the UNCLOS, it is mandatory that all local remedies of settlement and adjudication are exhausted and only after that international recourse of remediation must be sought under the UNCLOS III 1982, as specified under A.295 of the said Convention.

Article 279. of the UNCLOS III of 1982 obligates the disputing parties to settle their disputes by peaceful means. Part XV of the UNCLOS deals with the settlement of disputes.

Adjudicatory Bodies and Disputes Resolution Mechanism

1. Conciliation/Conciliatory Body

Conciliation is also one of the modes of a peaceful settlement. Once the parties agree to settle the dispute by conciliation in compliance with A.284 of the UNCLOS III of 1982.

When a conciliation procedure is sought a conciliatory body of 5 members is established for the purpose of resolving the dispute. The parties are bound to the rules established in the conciliatory process. However, if one of the parties has not consented to resolve the matter by conciliation at its inception then the parties are not bound by it and may opt for the other existing modes of adjudicating their dispute.

However, if the parties agree to resolve the dispute by conciliation, the conciliation committee/commission is formed of at least 5 members and the matter is taken up. Each party may propose two members to form the panel and one may be an independent member. The conciliation commission shall hear the parties, and elicit evidence and relevant documents in the process so as to help them to arrive at a conclusion. The commission shall resolve the dispute within 12 months and prepare a report of conciliation.

Example- The maritime boundary dispute between Timor-Leste and Australia was initiated in 2016 under the Law of the Sea and is regarded as the first case of conciliation under the new law.

Article 284 of UNCLOS III refers to the provision relating to Conciliation. It states-

"1. A State Party which is a party to a dispute concerning the interpretation or application of this Convention may invite the other party or parties to submit the dispute to conciliation in accordance with the procedure under Annex V, section 1, or another conciliation procedure.

2. If the invitation is accepted and if the parties agree upon the conciliation procedure to be applied, any party may submit the dispute to that procedure.

3. If the invitation is not accepted or the parties do not agree upon the procedure, the conciliation proceedings shall be deemed to be terminated.

2. The International Tribunal for the Law of the Sea (ITLOS)

ITLOS is an international body of adjudication to adjudicate disputes pertaining to the contravention of UNCLOS, and the allied disputes, specializing in the interpretation of the law of the Sea. The tribunal is set up under UNCLOS III in Hamburg Germany, which consists of 21 members with distinguished expertise in the Law of the Sea.

3. The International Court of Justice – ICJ

The ICJ is a general international court that handles matters even disputes under the Law of the Sea. The ICJ is composed of 15 members and they are appointed by the Security Council of the UN.

4. The General Arbitral Tribunal

Arbitral Tribunal is established to resolve disputes under the Law of the Sea. It is established under Annexure-VII of the Law of the Sea Convention.

The arbitral tribunal is composed of five members. Each party appoints one member and the first two members agree on appointing three additional members. Of the members appointed one of them shall be appointed as president of the tribunal.

Every dispute will be addressed by a new tribunal formed for that particular dispute and new members will be appointed for that purpose. The decisions are made by majority vote, with a quorum of at least 50 % of the members present, and, in case of a tie, the president shall have a veto vote and his additional vote shall settle the case and provide a binding decision.

4. The Special Arbitral Tribunal – SAT

SAT is established to resolve special matters related to fisheries, or matters relating to marine environment conservation, protection, pollution, etc. For the purpose of resolving the disputes, 5 members need to be appointed out of the 21-member specialized expert list maintained by t relevant agencies of the UN in that area. Each disputing State Party may choose 2 members of the list.

Conclusion

The decision of the tribunals established under the Law of the Sea operate as persuasive precedents and not binding precedents.

Article 287- provides for modes of resolving the disputes

It reads -

"1. When signing, ratifying or acceding to this Convention or at any time thereafter, a State shall be free to choose, by means of a written declaration, one or more of the following means for the settlement of disputes concerning the interpretation or application of this Convention:

(a) the International Tribunal for the Law of the Sea established in accordance with Annex VI;

(b) the International Court of Justice;

(c) an arbitral tribunal constituted in accordance with Annex VII;

(d) a special arbitral tribunal constituted in accordance with Annex VII for one or more of the categories of disputes specified therein.

2. A declaration made under paragraph I shall not affect or be affected by the obligation of a State Party to accept the jurisdiction of the Sea-Bed Disputes Chamber of the International Tribunal for the Law of the Sea to the extent and in the manner provided for in Part Xl, section 5."

Part XI – Section 5 deals with the Settlement of disputes and advisory opinions, and provides for the establishment of the Sea Bed Chamber Disputes Tribunal.

A. 287 further reads-

".....3. A State Party, which is a party to a dispute not covered by a declaration in force, shall be deemed to have accepted arbitration in accordance with Annex VII.

4. If the parties to a dispute have accepted the same procedure for the settlement of the dispute, it may be submitted only to that procedure, unless the parties otherwise agree.

5. If the parties to a dispute have not accepted the same procedure for the settlement of the dispute, it may be submitted only to arbitration in accordance with Annex VII, unless the parties otherwise agree.

6. A declaration made under paragraph 1 shall remain in force until three months after notice of revocation has been deposited with the Secretary General of the United Nations.

7. A new declaration, a notice of revocation, or the expiry of a declaration does not in any way affect proceedings pending before a court or tribunal having jurisdiction under this article unless the parties otherwise agree.

8. Declarations and notices referred to in this article shall be deposited with the Secretary-General of the United Nations, who shall transmit copies thereof to the States Parties."

Article 288 deals with 'Jurisdiction'.

"1. A court or tribunal referred to in article 287 shall have jurisdiction over any dispute concerning the interpretation or application of this Convention which is submitted to it in accordance with this Part.

2. A court or tribunal referred to in article 287 shall also have jurisdiction over any dispute concerning the interpretation or application of an international agreement related to the purposes of this Convention, which Is submitted to it in accordance with the agreement.

3. The Sea-Bed Disputes Chamber of the International Tribunal for the Law of the Sea established in accordance with Annex VI, and any other chamber or arbitral tribunal referred to in Part XI, section 5, shall have jurisdiction in any matter which is submitted to it in accordance therewith.

4. In the event of a dispute as to whether a court or tribunal has jurisdiction, the matter shall be settled by the decision of that court or tribunal."

Article 289 deals with Experts appointed to the Tribunals.

It reads- "In any dispute involving scientific or technical matters, a court or tribunal exercising jurisdiction under this section may, at the request of a party or proprio motu, select in consultation with the parties no fewer than two scientific or technical experts chosen preferably from the relevant list prepared in accordance with Annex VIII, article 2, to sit with the court or tribunal but without the right to vote."

Article 292

Prompt release of vessels and crews

1. Where the authorities of a State Party have detained a vessel flying the nag of another State Party and it is alleged that the detaining State has not complied with the provisions of this Convention for the prompt release of the vessel or its crew upon the posting of a reasonable bond or other financial security, the question of release from detention may be submitted to any court or tribunal agreed upon by the parties or, failing such agreement within 10 days from the time of detention, to a court or tribunal accepted by the detaining State under article 287 or to the International Tribunal for the Law of the Sea, unless the parties otherwise agree.

2. The application for release may be made only by or on behalf of the flag State of the vessel.

3. The court or tribunal shall deal without delay with the application for release and shall deal only with the question of release, without prejudice to the merits of any case before the appropriate domestic forum against the vessel, its owner or its crew. The authorities of the detaining State remain competent to release the vessel or its crew at any time.

4. Upon the posting of the bond or other financial security determined by the court or tribunal, the authorities of the

detaining State shall comply promptly with the decision of the court or tribunal concerning the release of the vessel or its crew.

Article 293

Applicable law

The Article reads- "1. A court or tribunal having jurisdiction under this section shall apply this Convention and other rules of international law not incompatible with this Convention.

2. Paragraph I does not prejudice the power of the court or tribunal having jurisdiction under this section to decide a case ex aequo et bono, if the parties so agree."

Ex Aequo Et Bono is a Latin term that means the case shall be decided on principles that are just and fair or in accordance with the principles of justice, equity, and good conscience.

Article 296

Finality and binding force of decisions upon the parties to the dispute

"Any decision rendered by a court or tribunal having jurisdiction under this section shall be final and shall be complied with by all the parties to the dispute...."

Appendix 1

EXTRACT OF UNCLOS - High Seas

PART VII

HIGH SEAS

SECTION 1. GENERAL PROVISIONS

Article 86

Application of the provisions of this Part

The provisions of this Part apply to all parts of the sea that are not included in the exclusive economic zone, in the territorial sea or in the internal waters of a State, or in the archipelagic waters of an archipelagic State. This article does not entail any abridgement of the freedoms enjoyed by all States in the exclusive economic zone in accordance with article 58.

Article 87

Freedom of the high seas

1. The high seas are open to all States, whether coastal or land-locked. Freedom of the high seas is exercised under the conditions laid down by this Convention and by

other rules of international law. It comprises, inter alia, both for coastal and land-locked States:

(a) freedom of navigation;

(b) freedom of overflight;

(c) freedom to lay submarine cables and pipelines, subject to Part VI;

(d) freedom to construct artificial islands and other installations permitted under international law, subject to Part VI;

(e) freedom of fishing, subject to the conditions laid down in section 2;

(f) freedom of scientific research, subject to Parts VI and XIII.

2. These freedoms shall be exercised by all States with due regard for the interests of other States in their exercise of the freedom of the high seas, and also with due regard for the rights under this Convention with respect to activities in the Area.

Article 88

Reservation of the high seas for peaceful purposes

The high seas shall be reserved for peaceful purposes.

Article 89

Invalidity of claims of sovereignty over the high seas

No State may validly purport to subject any part of the high seas to its sovereignty.

Article 90

Right of navigation

Every State, whether coastal or land-locked, has the right to sail ships flying its flag on the high seas.

Article 91

Nationality of ships

1. Every State shall fix the conditions for the grant of its nationality to ships, for the registration of ships in its territory, and for the right to fly its flag. Ships have the nationality of the State whose flag they are entitled to fly. There must exist a genuine link between the State and the ship.

2. Every State shall issue to ships to which it has granted the right to fly its flag documents to that effect.

Article 92

Status of ships

1. Ships shall sail under the flag of one State only and, save in exceptional cases expressly provided for in international treaties or in this Convention, shall be subject to its exclusive jurisdiction on the high seas. A ship may not change its flag during a voyage or while in a port of call, save in the case of a real transfer of ownership or change of registry.

2. A ship which sails under the flags of two or more States, using them according to convenience, may not claim any of the nationalities in question with respect to any other State, and may be assimilated to a ship without nationality.

Article 93

Ships flying the flag of the United Nations, its specialized agencies and the International Atomic Energy Agency

The preceding articles do not prejudice the question of ships employed on the official service of the United Nations, its specialized agencies or the International Atomic Energy Agency, flying the flag of the organization.

Article 94

Duties of the flag State

1. Every State shall effectively exercise its jurisdiction and control in administrative, technical and social matters over ships flying its flag.

2. In particular every State shall:

(a) maintain a register of ships containing the names and particulars of ships flying its flag, except those which are excluded from generally accepted international regulations on account of their small size; and

(b) assume jurisdiction under its internal law over each ship flying its flag and its master, officers and crew in respect of administrative, technical and social matters concerning the ship.

3. Every State shall take such measures for ships flying its flag as are necessary to ensure safety at sea with regard, inter alia, to:

(a) the construction, equipment and seaworthiness of ships;

(b) the manning of ships, labour conditions and the training of crews, taking into account the applicable international instruments;

(c) the use of signals, the maintenance of communications and the prevention of collisions.

4. Such measures shall include those necessary to ensure:

(a) that each ship, before registration and thereafter at appropriate intervals, is surveyed by a qualified surveyor of ships, and has on board such charts, nautical publications and navigational equipment and instruments as are appropriate for the safe navigation of the ship;

(b) that each ship is in the charge of a master and officers who possess appropriate qualifications, in particular in seamanship, navigation, communications and marine engineering, and that the crew is appropriate in qualification and numbers for the type, size, machinery and equipment of the ship;

(c) that the master, officers and, to the extent appropriate, the crew are fully conversant with and required to observe the applicable international regulations concerning the safety of life at sea, the prevention of collisions, the prevention, reduction and control of marine pollution, and the maintenance of communications by radio.

5. In taking the measures called for in paragraphs 3 and 4 each State is required to conform to generally accepted international regulations, procedures and practices and to take any steps which may be necessary to secure their observance.

6. A State which has clear grounds to believe that proper jurisdiction and control with respect to a ship have not been exercised may report the facts to the flag State. Upon receiving such a report, the flag State shall investigate the matter and, if appropriate, take any action necessary to remedy the situation.

7. Each State shall cause an inquiry to be held by or before a suitably qualified person or persons into every marine casualty or incident of navigation on the high seas involving a ship flying its flag and causing loss of life or serious injury to nationals of another State or serious damage to ships or installations of another State or to the marine environment. The flag State and the other State shall cooperate in the conduct of any inquiry held by that other State into any such marine casualty or incident of navigation.

Article 95

Immunity of warships on the high seas

Warships on the high seas have complete immunity from the jurisdiction of any State other than the flag State.

Article 96

Immunity of ships used only on government non-commercial service

Ships owned or operated by a State and used only on government non-commercial service shall, on the high seas, have complete immunity from the jurisdiction of any State other than the flag State.

Article 97

Penal jurisdiction in matters of collision or any other incident of navigation

1. In the event of a collision or any other incident of navigation concerning a ship on the high seas, involving the penal or disciplinary responsibility of the master or of any other person in the service of the ship, no penal or disciplinary proceedings may be instituted against such person except before the judicial or administrative authorities either of the flag State or of the State of which such person is a national.

2. In disciplinary matters, the State which has issued a master's certificate or a certificate of competence or licence shall alone be competent, after due legal process, to pronounce the withdrawal of such certificates, even if the holder is not a national of the State which issued them.

3. No arrest or detention of the ship, even as a measure of investigation, shall be ordered by any authorities other than those of the flag State.

Article 98

Duty to render assistance

1. Every State shall require the master of a ship flying its flag, in so far as he can do so without serious danger to the ship, the crew or the passengers:

(a) to render assistance to any person found at sea in danger of being lost;

(b) to proceed with all possible speed to the rescue of persons in distress, if informed of their need of assistance, in so far as such action may reasonably be expected of him;

(c) after a collision, to render assistance to the other ship, its crew and its passengers and, where possible, to inform the other ship of the name of his own ship, its port of registry and the nearest port at which it will call.

2. Every coastal State shall promote the establishment, operation and maintenance of an adequate and effective search and rescue service regarding safety on and over the sea and, where circumstances so require, by way of mutual regional arrangements cooperate with neighbouring States for this purpose.

Article 99

Prohibition of the transport of slaves

Every State shall take effective measures to prevent and punish the transport of slaves in ships authorized to fly its flag and to prevent the unlawful use of its flag for that purpose. Any slave taking refuge on board any ship, whatever its flag, shall ipso facto be free.

Article 100

Duty to cooperate in the repression of piracy

All States shall cooperate to the fullest possible extent in the repression of piracy on the high seas or in any other place outside the jurisdiction of any State.

Article 101

Definition of piracy

Piracy consists of any of the following acts:

(a) any illegal acts of violence or detention, or any act of depredation, committed for private ends by the crew or the passengers of a private ship or a private aircraft, and directed:

(i) on the high seas, against another ship or aircraft, or against persons or property on board such ship or aircraft;

(ii) against a ship, aircraft, persons or property in a place outside the jurisdiction of any State;

(b) any act of voluntary participation in the operation of a ship or of an aircraft with knowledge of facts making it a pirate ship or aircraft;

(c) any act of inciting or of intentionally facilitating an act described in subparagraph (a) or (b).

Article 102

Piracy by a warship, government ship or government aircraft whose crew has mutinied

The acts of piracy, as defined in article 101, committed by a warship, government ship or government aircraft whose crew has mutinied and taken control of the ship or aircraft are assimilated to acts committed by a private ship or aircraft.

Article 103

Definition of a pirate ship or aircraft

A ship or aircraft is considered a pirate ship or aircraft if it is intended by the persons in dominant control to be used for the purpose of committing one of the acts referred to in article 101. The same applies if the ship or aircraft has been used to commit any such act, so long as it remains under the control of the persons guilty of that act.

Article 104

Retention or loss of the nationality of a pirate ship or aircraft

A ship or aircraft may retain its nationality although it has become a pirate ship or aircraft. The retention or loss of nationality is determined by the law of the State from which such nationality was derived.

Article 105

Seizure of a pirate ship or aircraft

On the high seas, or in any other place outside the jurisdiction of any State, every State may seize a pirate ship or aircraft, or a ship or aircraft taken by piracy and under the control of pirates, and arrest the persons and seize the property on board. The courts of the State which carried out the seizure may decide upon the penalties to be imposed, and may also determine the action to be taken with regard to the ships, aircraft or property, subject to the rights of third parties acting in good faith.

Article 106

Liability for seizure without adequate grounds

Where the seizure of a ship or aircraft on suspicion of piracy has been effected without adequate grounds, the State making the seizure shall be liable to the State the nationality of which is possessed by the ship or aircraft for any loss or damage caused by the seizure.

Article 107

Ships and aircraft which are entitled to seize on account of piracy

A seizure on account of piracy may be carried out only by warships or military aircraft, or other ships or aircraft clearly marked and identifiable as being on government service and authorized to that effect.

Article 108

Illicit traffic in narcotic drugs or psychotropic substances

1. All States shall cooperate in the suppression of illicit traffic in narcotic drugs and psychotropic substances engaged in by ships on the high seas contrary to international conventions.

2. Any State which has reasonable grounds for believing that a ship flying its flag is engaged in illicit traffic in narcotic drugs or psychotropic substances may request the cooperation of other States to suppress such traffic.

Article 109

Unauthorized broadcasting from the high seas

1. All States shall cooperate in the suppression of unauthorized broadcasting from the high seas.

2. For the purposes of this Convention, "unauthorized broadcasting" means the transmission of sound radio or television broadcasts from a ship or installation on the high seas intended for reception by the general public contrary to international regulations, but excluding the transmission of distress calls.

3. Any person engaged in unauthorized broadcasting may be prosecuted before the court of:

(a) the flag State of the ship;

(b) the State of registry of the installation;

(c) the State of which the person is a national;

(d) any State where the transmissions can be received; or

(e) any State where authorized radio communication is suffering interference.

4. On the high seas, a State having jurisdiction in accordance with paragraph 3 may, in conformity with article 110, arrest any person or ship engaged in unauthorized broadcasting and seize the broadcasting apparatus.

Article 110

Right of visit

1. Except where acts of interference derive from powers conferred by treaty, a warship which encounters on the high seas a foreign ship, other than a ship entitled to complete immunity in accordance with articles 95 and 96, is not justified in boarding it unless there is reasonable ground for suspecting that:

(a) the ship is engaged in piracy;

(b) the ship is engaged in the slave trade;

(c) the ship is engaged in unauthorized broadcasting and the flag State of the warship has jurisdiction under article 109;

(d) the ship is without nationality; or

(e) though flying a foreign flag or refusing to show its flag, the ship is, in reality, of the same nationality as the warship.

2. In the cases provided for in paragraph 1, the warship may proceed to verify the ship's right to fly its flag. To this end, it may send a boat under the command of an officer to the suspected ship. If suspicion remains after the documents have been checked, it may proceed to a further examination on board the ship, which must be carried out with all possible consideration.

3. If the suspicions prove to be unfounded, and provided that the ship boarded has not committed any act justifying them, it shall be compensated for any loss or damage that may have been sustained.

4. These provisions apply mutatis mutandis to military aircraft.

5. These provisions also apply to any other duly authorized ships or aircraft clearly marked and identifiable as being on government service.

Article 111

Right of hot pursuit

1. The hot pursuit of a foreign ship may be undertaken when the competent authorities of the coastal State have good reason to believe that the ship has violated the laws and regulations of that State. Such pursuit must be commenced when the foreign ship or one of

its boats is within the internal waters, the archipelagic waters, the territorial sea or the contiguous zone of the pursuing State, and may only be continued outside the territorial sea or the contiguous zone if the pursuit has not been interrupted. It is not necessary that, at the time when the foreign ship within the territorial sea or the contiguous zone receives the order to stop, the ship giving the order should likewise be within the territorial sea or the contiguous zone. If the foreign ship is within a contiguous zone, as defined in article 33, the pursuit may only be undertaken if there has been a violation of the rights for the protection of which the zone was established.

2. The right of hot pursuit shall apply mutatis mutandis to violations in the exclusive economic zone or on the continental shelf, including safety zones around continental shelf installations, of the laws and regulations of the coastal State applicable in accordance with this Convention to the exclusive economic zone or the continental shelf, including such safety zones.

3. The right of hot pursuit ceases as soon as the ship pursued enters the territorial sea of its own State or of a third State.

4. Hot pursuit is not deemed to have begun unless the pursuing ship has satisfied itself by such practicable means as may be available that the ship pursued or one of its boats or other craft working as a team and using the ship pursued as a mother ship is within the limits of the territorial sea, or, as the case may be, within the

contiguous zone or the exclusive economic zone or above the continental shelf. The pursuit may only be commenced after a visual or auditory signal to stop has been given at a distance which enables it to be seen or heard by the foreign ship.

5. The right of hot pursuit may be exercised only by warships or military aircraft, or other ships or aircraft clearly marked and identifiable as being on government service and authorized to that effect.

6. Where hot pursuit is effected by an aircraft:

(a) the provisions of paragraphs 1 to 4 shall apply mutatis mutandis;

(b) the aircraft giving the order to stop must itself actively pursue the ship until a ship or another aircraft of the coastal State, summoned by the aircraft, arrives to take over the pursuit, unless the aircraft is itself able to arrest the ship. It does not suffice to justify an arrest outside the territorial sea that the ship was merely sighted by the aircraft as an offender or suspected offender, if it was not both ordered to stop and pursued by the aircraft itself or other aircraft or ships which continue the pursuit without interruption.

7. The release of a ship arrested within the jurisdiction of a State and escorted to a port of that State for the purposes of an inquiry before the competent authorities may not be claimed solely on the ground that the ship, in the course of its voyage, was escorted across a portion

of the exclusive economic zone or the high seas, if the circumstances rendered this necessary.

8. Where a ship has been stopped or arrested outside the territorial sea in circumstances which do not justify the exercise of the right of hot pursuit, it shall be compensated for any loss or damage that may have been thereby sustained.

Article 112

Right to lay submarine cables and pipelines

1. All States are entitled to lay submarine cables and pipelines on the bed of the high seas beyond the continental shelf.

2. Article 79, paragraph 5, applies to such cables and pipelines.

Article 113

Breaking or injury of a submarine cable or pipeline

Every State shall adopt the laws and regulations necessary to provide that the breaking or injury by a ship flying its flag or by a person subject to its jurisdiction of a submarine cable beneath the high seas done wilfully or through culpable negligence, in such a manner as to be liable to interrupt or obstruct telegraphic or telephonic communications, and similarly the breaking or injury of a submarine pipeline or high-voltage power cable, shall be a punishable offence. This provision shall apply also to conduct calculated or likely to result in such breaking or injury. However, it shall not apply to any break or injury caused by persons who acted merely with the legitimate object of saving their lives or their ships, after having taken all necessary precautions to avoid such break or injury.

Article 114

Breaking or injury by owners of a submarine cable or pipeline of another submarine cable or pipeline

Every State shall adopt the laws and regulations necessary to provide that, if persons subject to its jurisdiction who are the owners of a submarine cable or pipeline beneath the high seas, in laying or repairing that cable or pipeline, cause a break in or injury to another cable or pipeline, they shall bear the cost of the repairs.

Article 115

Indemnity for loss incurred in avoiding injury to a submarine cable or pipeline

Every State shall adopt the laws and regulations necessary to ensure that the owners of ships who can prove that they have sacrificed an anchor, a net or any other fishing gear, in order to avoid injuring a submarine cable or pipeline, shall be indemnified by the owner of the cable or pipeline, provided that the owner of the ship has taken all reasonable precautionary measures beforehand.

SECTION 2. CONSERVATION AND MANAGEMENT OF THE LIVING RESOURCES OF THE HIGH SEAS

Article 116

Right to fish on the high seas

All States have the right for their nationals to engage in fishing on the high seas subject to:

(a) their treaty obligations;

(b) the rights and duties as well as the interests of coastal States provided for, inter alia, in article 63, paragraph 2, and articles 64 to 67; and

(c) the provisions of this section.

Article 117

Duty of States to adopt with respect to their nationals measures for the conservation of the living resources of the high seas

All States have the duty to take, or to cooperate with other States in taking, such measures for their respective nationals as may be necessary for the conservation of the living resources of the high seas.

Article 118

Cooperation of States in the conservation and management of living resources

States shall cooperate with each other in the conservation and management of living resources in the areas of the high seas. States whose nationals exploit identical living resources, or different living resources in the same area, shall enter into negotiations with a view to taking the measures necessary for the conservation of the living resources concerned. They shall, as appropriate, cooperate to establish subregional or regional fisheries organizations to this end.

Article 119

Conservation of the living resources of the high seas

1. In determining the allowable catch and establishing other conservation measures for the living resources in the high seas, States shall:

(a) take measures which are designed, on the best scientific evidence available to the States concerned, to maintain or restore populations of harvested species at levels which can produce the maximum sustainable yield, as qualified by relevant environmental and economic factors, including the special requirements of developing States, and taking into account fishing patterns, the interdependence of stocks and any generally recommended international minimum standards, whether subregional, regional or global;

(b) take into consideration the effects on species associated with or dependent upon harvested species with a view to maintaining or restoring populations of such associated or dependent species above levels at which their reproduction may become seriously threatened.

2. Available scientific information, catch and fishing effort statistics, and other data relevant to the conservation of fish stocks shall be contributed and exchanged on a regular basis through competent international organizations, whether subregional, regional or global, where appropriate and with participation by all States concerned.

3. States concerned shall ensure that conservation measures and their implementation do not discriminate in form or in fact against the fishermen of any State.

Article 120

Marine mammals

Article 65 also applies to the conservation and management of marine mammals in the high seas.

Bibliography

- Draft Agreement Under the United Nations Convention on the Law of the Sea on the Conservation and Sustainable Use of Marine Biological Diversity of Areas Beyond National Jurisdiction (United Nations, 2023).
- Tzeng, Peter. Jurisdiction and Applicable Law Under UNCLOS. *The Yale Law Journal*, vol. 126, No. 1 (2016).
- Laikre, Linda, and others. Lack of Recognition of Genetic Biodiversity: International Policy and Its Implementation in Baltic Sea Marine Protected Areas. *Ambio*, vol. 45, No. 6 (2016).
- United Nations Convention on Law of the Sea.

About the Author

A Lawyer, Author, Faculty in Law, and a Human Rights Activist!

Ms. Henrietta Newton Martin (Henrietta Newton) is a Senior Legal Counsel by profession serving the corporate sector and has delivered lectures at leading universities and colleges internationally.

The author holds a Master of Laws Degree, in which she is a gold medallist, specializing in Human Rights and laws, she is a university topper, ranked first, and a gold medallist in her Bachelor of Laws as well. She has also done numerous courses transcending her area of practice, including special skills training in Human Resources Management and Administration. Henrietta Newton Martin is also a Bachelor of Commerce graduate- specializing in General/Personnel/Services Management. She has authored several books and articles in law and fiction. To know more about her and be updated on her latest releases, get connected and follow her on Twitter, Instagram, LinkedIn, Facebook, and Google.

Classroom Sessions on the Subject

For classroom sessions on the subject please use this url: www.youtube.com/@law-academicvideos

Notes

www.ingramcontent.com/pod-product-compliance
Ingram Content Group UK Ltd.
Pitfield, Milton Keynes, MK11 3LW, UK
UKHW060020051026
15591UKWH00006B/293